This book is dedicated in memory of my Dad,
and for Wendy, my number one supporter, who likes to
keep a copy of everything!

Photographs by Alex Foster and Kerry Wilkinson

Contents

6) Foreword by Cindy Carter of Resin Obsession

7) Introduction

8) What are the different types of resin, and why does it matter?

10) Useful tools and additives

15) Storage and Handling

17) Mixing

19) Sanding and Polishing

- PROJECTS -

22) Abalone shell necklace

25) Image keyrings

28) Fabric pendant

32) Leaf jewellery

36) Swirled dye bangle

39) Vintage decal pendant

43) Layering with glitter

47) Mould making

51) Using gelcoat as a glue

54) Ice jewellery

58) Swarovski highlights

62) Plique-a-jour bracelet

66) Troubleshooting

- GALLERY: INSPIRATIONAL ARTISTS -

68) Jasmine Scott

70) Deanna Buresco

72) Su Trindle

74) Serena Kuhl

76) Where to buy?

78) Index

Foreword
by Cindy Carter of ResinObsession

"How did you do that?" We just can't help ourselves. We see something new and we have to know how it's made. That's our creative spirit.

When we teach through books or the classroom not only do we allow an artist to grow but the teacher grows as well. I believe this is part of a cycle of artistic creativeness in the universe.

In this book, Kerry shares her discovery through her tutorials, the resin ice technique in particular contributes to this cycle. I'm sure we will see more from Kerry as she blossoms.

My obsession with resin came from a love of the translucency, sparkle and shine of glass. Resin gives me the opportunity to express my creative spirit using found items, memorabilia, and just about anything else one can imagine. As a self taught artist all other mediums seemed boring after a while but not resin- it's possibilities are endless. I'm very blessed to truly love what I do, my soul has found that special love- ResinObsession.

Cindy Carter founded and is currently running ResinObsession - a resin supply company- and the ResinObsession Blog,

Crafting with any type of medium imaginable has been a passion of Cindy's from the time she could add water to dirt to create elaborate mud pies. She first started working with resin while creating funky furniture pieces. She has a great job that she loves and is ready for wherever it takes her next.

Introduction

I have made jewellery for many years, but never before have I found a medium so versatile and rewarding as resin. As a fairly new craft in the UK, many people have contacted me for advice through the PennyDog website and the Crafteroo forum, and it is time that casting and creating contemporary yet classy plastic jewellery is given the prominence that it deserves, and the mystery that surrounds the process is put to rest.

Working with resin is not difficult, and most projects are relatively quick to complete. This book starts with simple projects for the beginner, moving on to other more intensive pieces, to help you develop your skills, offering troubleshooting tips and shortcuts along the way.

I hope you find the projects as aspiring as I did in creating them, and that you find the possibilities endless in developing your own unique style!

Kerry Wilkinson has experimented with various forms of jewellery making, experimenting in polymer clay, beadweaving and silver clay amongst other forms, and inventing her own processes and techniques along the way.

Through her education and occupational background, she has developed her skills, experience and appreciation of a variety of visual arts, including graphic and product design, which has influenced her jewellery work.

www.penny-dog.co.uk
www.crafteroo.co.uk

What are the different types of resin, and why does it matter?

There are two main resins used for crafting: polyester and epoxy. The difference between epoxy and polyester resins is in the chemical makeup of the two materials. The epoxy polymer chain works in parallel, reacting chemically with the chain immediately adjacent, causing it to set and therefore there is minimal shrinkage. With the polyester chain a catalyst is used to cause the chemical reaction, working on each chain individually, hence the small amount of hardener needed when mixing in comparison to epoxy. By moving chain by chain, this causes some shrinkage.

All of the projects in this book are polyester resin based, but why? Here are the main properties and usual uses of each type.

EPOXY

Epoxy resin is a low odour and viscous resin, making it ideal for coatings. Epoxy resins are in limited supply in the UK, but the most

popular coating resin (also known as "doming resin" due to the effect it creates on a surface) used in crafts is Envirotex Lite. In the States in particular, epoxy casting resins are also available, such as Easy Cast. Envirotex stays flexible for quite a long time and therefore is unsuitable for casting.

To mix epoxy, the ratio of hardener to resin is typically 1:1, with little margin for error when measuring. Epoxy resin is generally more expensive to purchase and takes longer to set.

POLYESTER

Polyester requires good ventilation and a face mask when working, as it is extremely pungent. Both types of resin are toxic, so taking safety precautions when working with resin of any type is essential. Amongst other suspicions, exposure can lead to narcosis, respiratory system irritation and liver and nerve damage. Polyester resin is the most widely used type for a variety of different applications, and is up to half the price of epoxy as it is used for industrial purposes and requires minimal catalyst (methyl ethyl ketone peroxide), typically 1-3% of the weight. It is available in both standard (tinted) and water clear varieties, which is more useful for embedding crafts and it sets much quicker than epoxy.

GELCOAT

Gelcoat is generally used in fibreglassing, though it has lots of useful applications in jewellery making, for filling or using as a glue (see page 51-53). It is usually a tinted solution and is almost paste-like, making it easy to apply without it running onto your work.

Almost clear versions are also available, which is best for making repairs to your jewellery work. Pigments can be added in the usual way. Your gelcoat should match the type of resin chosen (i.e. polyester gelcoat for polyester resin), otherwise it can start to separate. It is mixed in similar quantities to its comparative resin.

Useful tools and additives

When using resin, there are some extra things you will need that are essential, such as mixing equipment, and some things that can enhance your work, such as dyes and pigments. These will appear in the Projects section, so it is a good idea to familiarise yourself with the various tools and additives before getting down to work.

DISPOSABLE CUPS

It is nearly impossible to clean resin out of it's mixing container, so using a vessel that is designed to be thrown away after use will make your projects easier. Make sure you avoid polystyrene versions though, as the resin will melt them. You can buy disposable cups from the supermarket or pound shop quite cheaply.

LOLLY STICKS

Disposable sticks are also recommended to mix with for the same reason. Lolly sticks can be bought in packs of 100 or more from craft shops and also eBay, used for a variety of children's crafts, as well as making lollies. These are ideal for stirring.

MOULDS

There are different types of moulds available that you can use, some more flexible than others. Depending on the material, some moulds can be used as they are, though others may require a release agent. The smoothness and shine of the mould will affect the surface of the resin, as it will replicate it exactly. If you want a shiny casting, you need a shiny mould.

Polyethylene and Polypropylene: These moulds require no mould release, and all of the pre-made mould projects in this book use this type as it is ideal for the beginner and gives instant results. They are very flexible and can be reused many times because of this, making them brilliant value for money.

Chocolate/soap making moulds: With rigid moulds such as these, a release agent is recommended. Mould release wax is a good choice for jewellery making because it can be polished to a high sheen if this is the desired final effect. The resin tends to react with the harder plastic more during the curing process and will start to dull the surface, making release more difficult as well as creating more matte effect pieces. Generally these moulds can only be used three or four times before they are exhausted.

Silicone and Latex rubber:
These moulds are really flexible, so can produce more detailed castings and rarely demand mould release agents. Latex isn't recommended for large castings as it can interfere with the curing process, but can still give nice results for shallow jewellery pieces. These are the kinds of

moulds that you can make yourself, see pages 47-50. Also included in this category are silicone ice cube trays, which can be bought from most homewares retailers.

MOULD RELEASE

This is useful for using the harder plastic moulds, or casting within less flexible vessels, and especially useful if you use epoxy resin, rather than polyester. There are three types of mould release: wax, liquid and spray. If you can find a supplier for the spray on type, this is the best, most evenly applied method. Apply to the mould and allow to dry before pouring resin into the mould.

DYES AND PIGMENTS

Resin colourants come in two different forms, liquid and paste.

They are both concentrated substances, so less than 5% of weight is needed for a strong colour. If too much of either is added, it can hinder the curing process. The liquid types are available in transparent and opaque colours, and there is even a pearlescent dye available on the market.

Dye: This is the liquid stuff, which typically comes in a bottle with a dropper style dispensing system.

It often needs shaking before use, as it can separate and leave a clear syrup on the top. The range is quite limited, with only one shade of each colour available to buy, but you can mix them to create your own shade, just like paints.

Pigment: The tubs of paste are more widely available than the dyes, through specialist fibreglass and modelling companies, rather than craft retailers, but are usually in opaque colours only. They come in a huge array of different shades. They last a lot longer than dyes as less is needed, typically 1% of weight or even less. A little really does go a long way.

GLITTER

For evenly distributed glitter in your piece, the finer the better. Larger grain glitter would need applying in layers for the same effect. You can also use metallic embossing powders for a sparkly effect. This is still effective when mixed with translucent resin dyes.

SANDPAPER AND FILES

Wet and dry papers are the best for resin- especially the finer grades- as it is quite a soft plastic and easy to sand, and harsher abrasives will damage the surface. Don't skip grades, or the pieces will not be so transparent as a result, starting at grade 240 up to 1500 should be ideal, see page 19-20 for more information.

CAR LACQUER SPRAY

For instant shine, car lacquer can really boost your piece once sanded. Some people recommend painting another layer of resin over the top, but this is the less messy option. It can chip off if the layers are too thick, so a couple of coats should be enough for even coverage. Available from most car accessory shops in the paint section, which is also where you should be able to pick up your wet and dry sandpapers quite easily.

DRILL AND DRILL BITS

A normal power drill, or a good power multi tool (such as a Dremel) will do the job, but a bench drill, or a stand for your drill is even better as it will ensure accurate and straight holes in your pieces for a more professional finish. Thinner drill bits will create smaller and neater bore holes, but sometimes a slightly bigger one is necessary for the job in hand.

PLIERS

For opening and closing jump rings, two pairs of pliers are recommended, one to hold each side of the ring. If you have soft metal jump rings you can do it with one pair, and substitute the other pair for your fingers. Smaller pliers, such as these needle-nosed ones are suited for the job as they don't obscure the view of what you are doing.

Storage and Handling

Working with resin can cause multiple health problems, so should be used with caution and care. It's also difficult to clean, so it's best to prepare yourself for spillages too.

VENTILATION

The most important piece of kit that you will need is a face mask with a ventilator. Dust masks are not enough when working with it in liquid or gelcoat form, as it releases Styrene fumes, which can cause respiratory problems, and there is some concern that this can further lead to lung cancer. If possible, work with it in a garage or workshop rather than in a domestic setting. Polyester resin smells strongly, and it isn't pleasant, and the smell will linger long after the fumes have dissipated.

When sanding resin, the dust is also very harmful for the same reasons, though without the fumes. A dust mask should be worn at this stage to prevent particles from entering your lungs. When working in either of these conditions, ensure there is good air circulation: open windows so there is a thoroughfare of clean air.

PROTECTION

As resin is very sticky, and water resistant, prevention is easier than the cure. Cover your work surfaces with clingfilm, which will allow you to throw away any spillages once cured. Polythene sheeting is reusable, as any droplets of hard resin can be peeled away afterwards. Wearing an apron is also advisable to protect your clothes.

To protect your skin, you can get latex gloves, which are also reuseable as the resin will not stick permanently to them. These are particularly useful as resin can create a water resistant coating on your hands, which cannot be removed by soap. If you do get a spillage on a surface, or on your skin, you can use rags soaked in nail varnish remover to remove it.

STORAGE

Even with a sealed container, store your resin upright as it is known to leak on occasion. It will normally keep for 3 months. It should be kept below 20°C, much higher and the longevity reduces and any higher than 30°C and it becomes a fire risk, as resin is highly flammable. Nail varnish remover and catalyst are also flammable substances, and it is recommended that they are stored in a cool, dark place away from direct sunlight.

DISPOSAL

Don't pour liquid resin down the drain as it may block and contribute to environmental issues, instead wait for it to cure in the mixing container then it can be safely thrown into the bin. If you can remove it from the cup, the cup can then be recycled by yourself for future batches, or recycled where facilities are available.

Mixing

1) An easy way to measure how much resin you will need for your projects is to fill the mould with water and pour into a disposable cup, marking where the water line is with a permanent marker pen.

2) Empty the water away and dry your mould and cup thoroughly.

3) Put the cup on some kitchen scales and zero the weight to eliminate the weight of the cup.

4) Fill the cup with resin up to the marker line and weigh. Pour in close to the cup so not to trap any unwanted air.

17

5) Work out the desired percentage of catalyst, for example for 3% of the weight, take the displayed figure (e.g. 45g) then divide by 100 and multiply by 3; *45÷100= 0.45, x3= 1.35g catalyst.*

6) Add the required catalyst to the cup. You can do this by measuring the amount with a disposable syringe or small medicine measuring cup (don't use for any other purpose once used for catalyst!). If you have a dropper bottle style dispenser, 30 drops is approximately 1ml, so for our example of 45g, you would need to add around 40 drops.

7) Mix very thoroughly for at least one full minute, scraping the edges and making sure not to whip the mixture as this adds bubbles.At about 20°C temperature, 3% catalyst addition will allow for around 10 minutes pot life (or working time before it begins curing), lower amounts and temperatures give a longer working time.

Sanding and Polishing

There are two ways of sanding, which goes hand in hand with polishing. You can sand by hand, or you can use a grinder designed for glass. Make sure you wear a dust mask for both kinds of sanding.

HAND SANDING

The most important thing to remember is to work your way through the grades for the smoothest and most flawless finish. The lower the number on the sandpaper, the coarser it is. Start from coarse and work your way up to fine. You may need to start filing the piece with metal files before going onto the sandpaper stage if there is a lot of surplus on the piece. If you sand it wet, the paper will become less clogged and less dust particles will enter the air. It is recommended that your final stage is done wet as it also produces a finer finish. After sanding, you may wish to progress onto steel wool, which will help make the piece look more glossy. Finally if you are sanding a transparent piece and it is looking a little cloudy, try using some T-Cut on a piece of cotton to buff the surface before moving onto polishing. If you would like a more matte finish, rub a little linseed oil or hand cream into the surface to bring out the colour.

MACHINE SANDING

Sanding using a flat lap grinder requires you to wear eye protection also. These machine have changeable grade disks. The two most useful grades for resin are 600 and 1200 as any coarser and it will cut too fast. The cutting speed is variable on the machine and

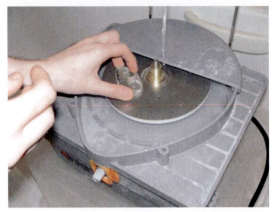

should be kept low at all times as resin is a soft material. You can add Diamond Coolant to the water reservoir which will preserve the disks for longer and also reduce the cutting speed for better control. Set your machine up outside, or in a bathroom, as things can get a bit wet. Be cautious of your electrical supply- ensure the two never meet.

POLISHING WITH A BUFFING WHEEL

You can get buffing wheels (or polishing mops) that attach to power drills and multi tool devices, so you don't need to spend a lot of money on a dedicated machine. Hold your piece downwards at 45° against the wheel, at the side where the travel is from top to bottom. You don't need to press too hard, again due to the softness of the material. If this happens, the heat can cause the piece to melt slightly and pieces of cotton may get stuck. This will need to be sanded off before attempting again.

MACHINE POLISHING

You can also get polishing wheels for flat lap machines, and in some cases they may come as part of the original set up. Disconnect the water reservoir before using, and apply liquid polishing compound to the disk with a sponge. Switch on the machine to low power and operate as with the buffing wheel, don't apply too much pressure.

Projects

Abalone shell necklace

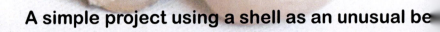

A simple project using a shell as an unusual be

A small amount of resin can turn a shell into a unique neckpiece, embedding starfish, smaller shells or even pearl effect beads for a delicate oyster effect.

YOU WILL NEED

Small abalone shell
(approximately 5cm in length)

Miniature starfish
(approximately 1cm in diameter)

Water clear polyester resin

1 6mm plated silver clamp

1 sterling silver chain

needle nosed pliers

disposable cup

lolly stick

1) Arrange your starfish inside the concave of the shell.

3) Drip the resin carefully into the shell using the mixing stick. Make sure not to let it get too full, or the resin will leak out of the holes in the shell. Leave to cure for 36 hours.

2) Mix the resin with catalyst at 3% of weight as more is required for shallow casting.

23

4) Attach the clamp through a naturally occuring hole close to the top of the shell and close with pliers, making sure not to put pressure on the shell as it will break.

Tip...

If the resin in the shell dulls, you can revive it with a speck of linseed or olive oil on a cloth. Polish the surface with the oil, then polish it with bare cloth to bring back the shine.

5) Thread your chain through the clamp to complete your necklace.

Image keyrings

Preparing and using images to create flexible graphic pieces

Use homebrew new bottlecaps or recycle your old ones to create your own keyrings with your favourite images.

1) Cut out your image to fit inside the bottlecap. This is usually 1 inch in diameter.

2) Coat image with a thin but thorough layer of glue and leave to dry.

YOU WILL NEED

A clean flat bottlecap

A printed image

Scissors

Disposable cup

Lolly stick

PVA glue and small paintbrush

Water clear polyester resin

1 13mm plated silver clamp

1 keyring / large split ring

needle nosed pliers

A power drill with 3mm drill bit

3) Put a drop of glue inside the bottlecap and place the image on top.

4) Squeeze from the centre outwards so that glue is visible around the edge of the image to seal in the edges. Leave to dry overnight.

5) Mix resin with catalyst at 3% of weight and pour into the bottlecap up to the top. Leave for 48 hours.

6) Drill a hole towards the top of the bottlecap, working from behind. If piece becomes cloudy, spray with a thin layer of car lacquer.

7) Open the clamp with the pliers and attach the keyring.

8) Clamp shut with pliers through the drilled hole.

Tip...

If you cut slightly smaller than the inside of the bottlecap, the resin will hold onto the cap too, rather than just the paper which will allow for a better hold when drilling.

Fabric pendant

Recycle old clothes or use your favourite fabrics to create unique jewellery

Designs are limited only to your fabric stash, and the process can be applied to bangles, earrings and rings too.

YOU WILL NEED
A mould
Fabric
Scissors
Water clear polyester resin
Disposable cup
Lolly stick
10mm wide organza ribbon
2 10mm ribbon clamps
4 6mm jump rings
1 lobster clasp
Pliers
Super glue gel
A power drill with 4mm drill bit
Wet and dry sandpaper (Grades 240, 400, 600 and 1500)
Car lacquer spray

1) Cut out your fabric to fit inside the mould.

2) Mix the resin with 2% catalyst (or as advised on the container) in a cup.

3) Pour a small amount into your mould, to fill it a third full. Place the fabric into the mould facing downwards.

4) Push down with the lolly stick to saturate the fabric. Work from the middle outwards, to push any trapped bubbles out from underneath it.

29

5) Fill the mould to the top with more resin and leave for at least 36 hours to allow it to set.

6) Once set, pop your resin out of the mould by pushing from underneath like an ice cube tray.

7) Sand rough edges with the lower grade sandpaper, and work your way through the other grades.

8) For the final grade, submerge your resin piece and the sandpaper in water when sanding for a finer finish.

9) Dry and spray with car lacquer to add a glossy sheen. Allow lacquer to dry before spraying the reverse.

10) Starting from the front, drill a hole through the pendant close to the top. Drill gradually in small bursts for a smooth hole.

11) Cut a piece of co-ordinating organza ribbon 18 inches in length.

12) Fold the ends of the ribbon over and attach the ribbon clamps tightly, one at each end.

13) Add a small amount of super glue gel along the teeth of the clamps for extra security.

14) With the ribbon folded in half, push the loop through the hole in the pendant, and put the ends of the ribbon through the loop creating a knot.

15) Add a jump ring and clasp to one end of the ribbon using the pliers. On the other end, add a 6mm jump ring and affix another, closing the first ring. Add another jump ring to the end of this to create an adjustable length necklace.

Leaf jewellery

Create autumnal effects with metal leaf shreds

Use gold, silver or copper leaf alone or in combination to create unique earrings and a pendant with suspended colours.

1) Mix the resin with 3% catalyst (or as advised on the container) in a cup.

2) Fill the moulds half full. Scrape the stick of any excess resin.

3) The moisture on the stick will aid the tearing of the metal leaf sheet.

4) Add the leaf to the moulds with the lolly stick.

33

5) Fill the rest of the moulds with the clear resin. You may need to manipulate the leaf inside slightly after doing this for a more appealing composition. Leave to set.

6) Once set, pop your pieces out of the moulds by pushing from underneath like an ice cube tray.

7) File the centre of the earring hoops with the needle file in a circular motion until the surplus has been removed.

8) Sand rough edges with the lower grade sandpaper, and work your way through the other grades.

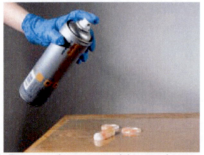

9) Dry and spray with car lacquer to add a glossy sheen. Allow lacquer to dry before spraying the reverse.

10) Open a 9mm jump ring, place through the loop in the earring piece and attach a 6mm jump ring. Close the ring.

11) Open a kidney wire and hook onto the 6mm jump ring, ensuring that the domed surface faces outwards when fastened. Repeat steps 10 and 11 for the second earring.

12) Drill a hole into the top of the pendant piece.

13) Super glue the peg into the hole, with the loop lying horizontally, and leave to dry.

14) Open the remaining 6mm jump ring and thread through the peg loop. Insert chain and close the ring.

Tip...

The best way to open and close jump rings is to pull one end forwards and the other backwards so not to distort the circle. This will reduce the stress on the metal and keep your connections strong. You can push the ends together slightly when closing if necessary.

Swirled dye bangle

Use one or two colours to create organically coloured wristwear

Try one or two colours to create bangles to match your wardrobe, no two will ever be identical!

1) Mix the resin thoroughly with 2% weight catalyst (or as advised on the container) in a cup, about 1/3rd full.

2) Add a small amount of dye. If in squeezy bottles, about 3-5 drops. With the paste types a lot less is needed, dip another lolly stick into the dye and place back in the cup.

3) Draw a circle in the cup twice with the lolly stick. The dye will not be thoroughly mixed, which is exactly the right effect.

4) Pour into the mould, working your way around so not to concentrate colour in only one area until filled. Leave to set for 36 hours.

37

5) Remove from the mould. You may need to turn the centre inside out in order to get a grip of the bangle.

6) Using the 250 grade sandpaper, work your way around the edge of the bangle so to remove the lip. Repeat for the inner circle.

7) Work your way through the other grades of wet and dry.

8) For the last grade, submerge in water whilst sanding for a smoother finish.

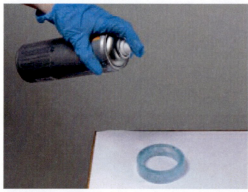

9) Spray with lacquer. Leave to dry. Rotate and spray again until evenly covered.

Tip...

You can mix one opaque colour in completely and swirl another colour inside for a bolder effect.

Vintage decal pendant

Combine opaque imagery with transparency for an unusual, effective pendant

Create a pendant that's both clear and opaque, with an easy to apply image inside.

1) Dampen decal and apply pressure to backing paper, before sliding the paper away to apply the decal to the acetate.

2) Cut acetate around the decal to the size of the mould. This tutorial uses a mould that measures 1" x 1.5".

3) Mix the resin thoroughly with 3% weight catalyst in a cup, about 1/6ths full.

Tip...

Make sure the acetate is completely dry before setting in resin. Resin resists water and will not set. Try putting it in the airing cupboard for a couple of hours to make sure.

4) Pour resin into the mould, filling it half full.

5) Place piece of acetate face down in the resin and push down so that resin flows over the top of the piece and removes any trapped bubbles.

6) Fill the rest of the mould with the clear resin and leave to set.

7) Pop the piece out of the mould.

8) Sand rough edges with the lower grade sandpaper, and work your way through the other grades.

9) For the last grade, submerge in water whilst sanding for a clearer finish.

41

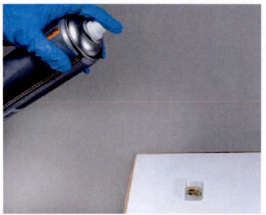

10) Spray with lacquer. Leave to dry. Rotate and spray again until evenly covered.

11) Drill slowly into the top of the piece, creating a hole approximately 3mm deep.

12) Put a small amount of superglue gel inside and around the hole. Insert the peg, with hole facing forward.

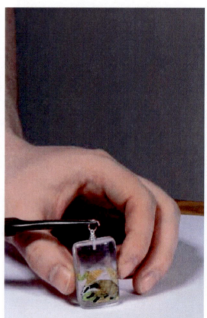

13) Once dry, open the jump ring and put through the hole in the peg. Close the ring.

14) Thread the chain through the jump ring to complete.

Layering
with glitter

**Use layering to create your own
3-dimensional mini collage necklaces**

So far, the projects have only used one layer of resin. Here's a project that uses three and unlocks the potential of layering!

YOU WILL NEED

A mould

Water clear polyester resin

Disposable cup

Lolly stick

Wet and dry sandpaper (Grades 240, 400, 600 and 1500)

A power drill with 1.5mm drill bit

Superglue Gel

Car lacquer spray

1 9mm plated peg

1 6mm jump ring

1 plated chain

Metallic stickers

Letter Beads

Glitter

1) Mix the resin with 3% catalyst (or as advised on the container) in a cup.

2) Pour a thin layer of resin into the mould, filling it about 1/5th.

Tip...

For layers one and two, you can use leftover catalysed resin from other projects as a way of reducing waste.

3) Float a sticker face down towards the bottom half of the mould (if using vertically) and leave to set.

4) Mix another batch of resin as before.

5) Pour into the mould, this time filling it just over half way.

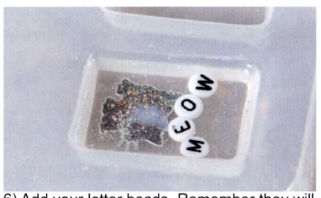

6) Add your letter beads. Remember they will need to be facing down and read backwards, you can check if you've got them the right way by carefully looking from the base of the mould. Leave to set.

7) Mix the last batch of resin. Add your glitter to the mix and stir well.

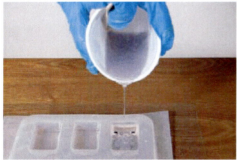

8) Pour into the mould up to the top and leave to set.

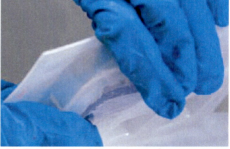

9) Pop the piece out of the mould.

10) Sand rough edges with the lower grade sandpaper, and work your way through the other grades.

11) For the last grade, submerge in water whilst sanding for a smoother finish.

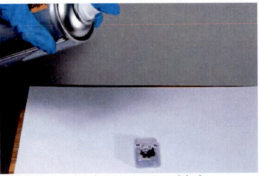

12) Dry well, then spray with lacquer. Leave to dry. Rotate and spray again until evenly covered.

13) Drill slowly into the top of the piece, creating a hole approximately 3mm deep.

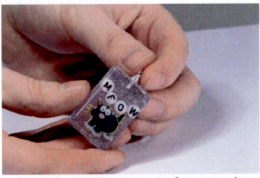

14) Put a small amount of super glue gel inside and around the hole. Insert the peg, with hole facing forward.

15) Once dry, open the jump ring and put through the hole in the peg. Close the ring. Thread chain through jump ring to complete.

Mould making

Introducing two mouldmaking materials and creating your own ring mould

The simplest of moulds, and one of the most useful for standard shape jewellery is the open mould, which is the type that is open at the back, just like the premade moulds used so far. There are two main moulding materials that can be used at home, Room Temperature Vulcanising (RTV) Silicone and Re-meltable PVC, which comes in the form of Vinamould or Gelflex. Other mould builders can be used, e.g. Latex, but it is only suitable for shallow casting.

RTV SILICONE

RTV silicone is moulded cold, and so is perfect for creating a mould from heat sensitive models, such as plastics and modelling materials (see next page). It is quite expensive to buy, but very user friendly and models and casting alike can be removed with ease. It works in a similar way to resin, a catalyst is added to start the curing process. Different speed catalysts  are available, and so mixing instructions vary, though catalyst is usually added in a ratio of 1:10.

VINAMOULD

 Vinamould is re-meltable and therefore reuseable. It is designed to be used with a melting pot and plate, but small pieces can be added to a thick tupperware container and put into the microwave for bursts of 30 seconds, pouring the liquid PVC over the model as it melts. If left for longer, it can overheat, turn brown and burn through your container. For best results, heat in one batch on a hot plate. It is not thought to be hazardous to health, but it does release unpleasant fumes, so if working with it in your kitchen, open your windows.

MILLIPUT AND MODELLING MATERIALS

You can create your own masters to mould from using many materials. Milliput is a favourite in the modelling world. It is a two part epoxy putty that you mix in even quantities and then model into the desired shape. It is easily filed and sanded, so that you can make it very smooth, ready for mould making. If the model is smooth, the resulting resin cast will be equally as smooth as silicone picks up every little detail in the surface. Other modelling materials such as polymer clay can be used, and even plastercine if used with care (see Serena Kuhl's work, page 74-75).

Here's how to make a simple band style ring mould using RTV silicone rubber.

1) Measure the container's length, width and height (up to 1cm extra on top of the height of the ring) in cm. If square or rectangular, multiply these numbers together to get the volume in ml. This is the amount of silicone you will need.

In this example it is a cylinder, so you need to measure the diameter of the base, divide by two to get the radius. Multiple the radius by itself (e.g. 2cm x 2cm= 4cm), then multiply by π (3.14) and multiply by the height.

2) Measure this amount in water in a measuring jug and pour into the disposable cup, marking the water line with a pen.

49

3) Empty the water and add the RTV silicone up to this line.

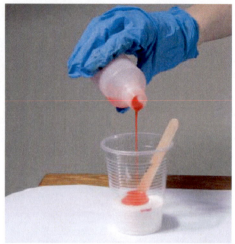

4) Add the catalyst at the ratio outlined on the product. This example is 10:1, so you would measure out 10% of the volume of silicone calculated in this instance.

5) Mix thoroughly, scraping the edges of the container inwards until it is a consistent colour.

6) Put the ring into the bottom of the container. Pour the silicone over the top in a thin stream to minimise trapped bubbles and leave to harden. It will take at least 24 hours for it to be completely cured.

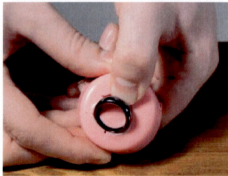

7) Pull the rubber out of the container, your ring should be easy to remove and now you can fill the mould with resin to create your own rings.

Using gelcoat as a glue

Any little trinkets can be turned into stud earrings, glitter, sequins, tiny stones, metal leaf and many other possibilities

Four tiny drops of resin and two tiny drops of gelcoat- a more viscous resin- can produce little gems for your ears!

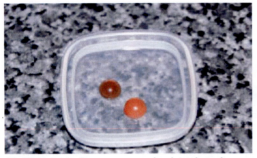

1) Put two 8mm rounded cabochons inside a small container facing upwards. Prepare the Vinamould as discussed on page 48.

2) Pour the Vinamould over the cabochons, allowing for an extra 5mm of depth once they are completely covered. Leave to cool.

3) Pull the rubber out of the container and remove the cabochons to produce your mould.

4) A tiny bit of resin is needed at this stage, so if you have some clear catalysed resin left over from another project, this is the time to use it! Drip one drop from the lolly stick into each part of the mould.

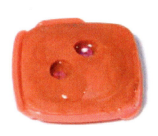

5) Put your intended inclusions into the moulds. It could be metal leaf, tiny beads, sequins or polymer clay.

6) Top up the mould, it should probably only take one more drip in each. Leave to cure.

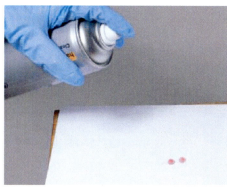

7) Pop the pieces out of the mould. File the rough edges with a needle file. Large amounts can be cut off with scissors.

8) Place the domes face up and give one coat of lacquer. Leave to dry and turn upside down.

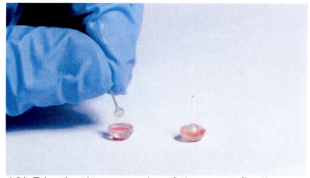

9) Mix the gelcoat with 3% catalyst. Only a small amount is needed.

10) Dip the base ends of the post findings into the gelcoat then place them onto the reverse of the resin pieces. Leave to set. Once dry you can add the clutches.

Ice
jewellery

This technique is actually very quick and simple, it is all about timing

Using a "mashing" technique, you can create imitation ice, or add colours to make imitation raw gemstones.

1) Mix the resin with 3% catalyst (or as advised on the container) in a cup. You will need about 1/5 of a cup full for 3 or 4 pieces.

2) Leave the cup for a while, the time can vary between 10 minutes and half an hour depending on the speed of the catalyst.

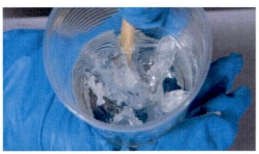

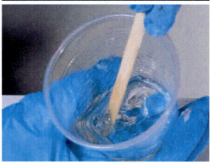

3) The resin in the cup will turn into a viscous gel. After this stage (about 3 minutes later) it will start to turn solid.

4) At this stage, use the lolly stick to cut it into pieces.

5) Turn the pieces out onto a plastic mat. Once on here they can be manipulated with the stick further. Leave to set.

6) Peel the pieces from the sheet. Put a small piece in the vice with a flat surface facing upwards.

7) Mix the gelcoat with 3% catalyst.

8) Drip a little onto the pad on the ring back, and place onto the resin piece.

9) Allow the gelcoat to overlap onto the back of the pad for extra grip and leave to set.

10) Drill slowly into the top of the pendant piece, creating a hole approximately 3mm deep.

11) Put a small amount of super glue gel inside and around the hole.

12) Insert the peg, with hole facing forward.

13) Once dry, open the jump ring and put through the hole in the peg.

14) Thread the chain through jump ring to complete.

Tip...

The pieces will dull a little after a while, you can paint a layer of resin over the top, and leave to dry, which will create a glossier finish.

Swarovski highlights

Add a touch of sparkle to a finished piece with chatons

Different stone colours and different colour resin shapes can be combined in many ways for differing effects. Use black or pearlescent colours for a sophisticated look.

YOU WILL NEED

Water clear polyester resin

A mould

Disposable cup

2 Lolly sticks

Black pigment

Clear Gelcoat

3 Swarovski chatons

Wet and dry sandpaper (Grades 240, 400, 600 and 1500)

Car lacquer spray

Pin

A power drill with 1.5mm drill bit

Pointed high speed steel cutter bit

Super glue gel

9mm peg

Pliers

6mm jump ring

Chain

1) Mix the resin with 3% catalyst (or as advised on the container) in a cup. You will need about 1/8 of a cup full.

2) Dip the second lolly stick into the black pigment and mix in with the resin thoroughly.

3) Pour into the mould and leave to set.

59

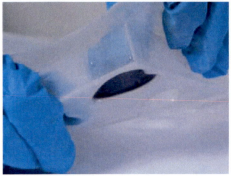

4) After 24-36 hours have passed, pop the piece out of the mould.

5) Sand the edges smooth with sandpaper, working your way through the grades from low to high.

6) Using the 1.5mm drill bit, drill a few shallow holes in the front of the piece where you would like to position the stones.

7) Attach the pointed cutter bit to the drill, and widen the holes, drilling to a depth of 3 or 4mm, or the depth of the point on the chaton.

8) Spray the piece evenly with acrylic lacquer and leave to dry.

9) Mix a small amount of gelcoat with 3% catalyst.

10) Apply a dot of gelcoat into each cavity with a pin.

11) Insert the chatons on top of the gelcoat, you may need tweezers to apply precisely. Leave for 6 hours.

12) With the 1.5mm drill bit attached, drill a hole in the top if the heart about 3mm deep.

13) Apply super glue around the hole and insert the peg. Leave to dry.

14) Open the jump ring and put through the hole in the peg. Close, and string chain through to complete.

Tip...

For these types of pegs, gluing can be tricky. Try drilling the hole in the top before adding the chatons, then- using the same gelcoat- dip the peg in and insert into hole.

Plique-a-jour bracelet

Recreate an enamelling technique using resin and acrylic.

This mixed media piece combines two plastics. Alternatively, use transparent colours for a stained glass effect.

1) Trace the template above onto a piece of thin paper.

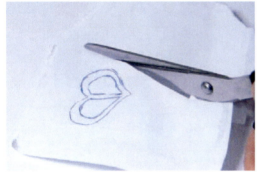

2) Roughly cut around the design.

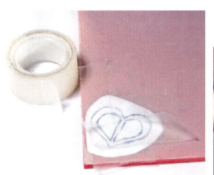

3) Using magic tape, stick the design onto the acrylic with a criss-cross pattern. Don't remove the film.

4) Clamp the acrylic in a vice and carefully cut around the outside with the piercing saw.

YOU WILL NEED

Water clear polyester resin

Dye of your choice

Disposable cup

Lolly stick

3mm thick acrylic sheet in colour of your choice

Piercing saw

Vice

Paper

Pencil

Magic tape

Wet and dry sandpaper (Grades 240, 400, 600 and 1500)

Needle file

A power drill with 1.5mm drill bit

Buffing wheel

Jeweller's Rouge

2 9mm jump rings

1 plated bracelet chain

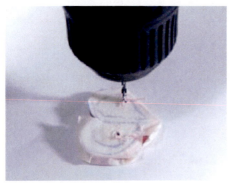

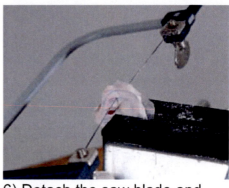

5) To cut out the inside details, drill a hole in the centre of your first half.

6) Detach the saw blade and reattach once threaded through the hole. Saw out detail and repeat for other side.

7) Remove any remaining paper, film and tape from your shape.

8) Apply magic tape in the same way as before on what will be the front of the shape, pressing firmly to ensure the holes are well covered.

9) Mix the resin thoroughly with 3% weight catalyst in a cup, and add dye to compliment the colour of acrylic.

Tip...

Before adding the second batch of tape, you can tidy up the edges with a needle file.

10) Drip the resin into the cut outs. You can use different batches of resin in different colours to suit. Leave to dry.

11) Once dry, peel tape from the reverse of the piece.

12) Smooth rough edges on your acrylic with a needle file. You may need to lightly sand the surface of your shape with fine wet and dry paper to remove any resin spills.

13) Drill a hole at either side of the heart.

14) Using a buffing wheel and jeweller's rouge, shine the front and back of the piece.

15) Attach the chain with jump rings through the drilled holes.

Troubleshooting

The resin is still tacky in the mould after 48 hours, what can I do?

Air hinders the curing process, so the resin that is covered by the mould will cure first which will allow it to be removed. If the back is still sticky, try leaving the piece in an airing cupboard or similar warm place overnight, as a gentle heat source encourages both polyester and epoxy catalysts. If you can make it airtight, then even better. Try putting the piece in a ziplock bag before putting it in a warm place.

The resin is stuck inside the mould, how can I get it out?

Put the mould inside a freezer for about half an hour, and then try pushing the piece out as normal. The cold encourages the resin to contract, and the slightly smaller size is easier to remove.

I have trapped bubbles in my piece, but it is still liquid- what can I do?

With a heat gun, lightly heat the surface of the resin. The bubbles will rise to the top as long as there are no inclusions blocking the way. Make sure not to apply heat for too long as resin can suddenly ignite under hot temperatures when still liquid. If the bubbles are close to the surface, you can burst them with a cocktail stick by

touching the bubble and drawing it out from the surface.

I have trapped bubbles in my piece but it has hardened- what can I do?

Some bubbles if well placed can be drilled into to attach a peg bail for fastening to jewellery. If they create a hole in the surface and is in a reasonably inconspicuous place, you can fill the holes with gelcoat, allow to dry, then file down to be level with the rest of the piece. Unfortunately large bubbles in the middle of a design cannot be fixed and in some cases will go to waste, though if they don't break the surface you may decide that they add to the uniqueness of the piece.

How do I know if something will float or sink in the resin?

If a piece sinks, you will need to cast a layer first before adding the inclusion so that it does not protrude through the surface, and if it floats you will want to add a layer afterwards so your object isn't too far back in the piece. This can be tested by seeing whether the item floats or sinks in water, and the same will apply to resin.

Can I embed flowers and insects?

Yes, but they must be dried first as moisture interferes with curing resin. Store specimens with silica gel for a few weeks, and try pressing flowers first. It is also recommended that you look out for bio resin as standard water clear resin can drain the colours. Bio resin is used for paperweights and is available through hobby modelling suppliers.

I want to create a mould of a rubber object, is this possible?

Yes but you will need to use RTV Silicone and a release agent. Apply a mixture of 1 part white spirit to 1 part vaseline to the surface of the item to be moulded before pouring on your new batch of silicone.

I have chipped the lacquer coating on a finished piece, how can I repair it and is there an alternative?

Sand off the remaining lacquer. You can add a tiny amount of catalysed resin to a paper towel and use as a polish to buff the surface. Leave to set. You can also use polishing compounds as described on page 19.

Gallery
Inspirational Artists

Jasmine Scott

Originally from New Zealand, Jasmine Scott currently lives and works in St Augustine, Florida USA. She studied at the prestigious National Art School, Sydney, Australia. Over the years Scott has moved from a dark figurative oeuvre to more vibrantly colored abstracts, which have further evolved into a dynamic collection of whimsical rings. Inspiration is derived from a love for candy and all things retro and fun. Minimalist and playful, these rings have a universal appeal. Through meticulous workings, the rings capture a vibrancy of light with their luxurious and resilient colors. From the striking to the subtle, she has managed to create a marriage of modern design with artistic expression in a stylish and ultimately wearable work of art.

"Sugar"
photograph courtesy of J. Scott

"Cognac"
photograph courtesy of J. Scott

"Urchin"
photograph courtesy of J. Scott

"Amaretto"
photograph courtesy of J. Scott

Gallery
Inspirational Artists

Deanna Burasco

Deanna Burasco studied art and advertising at Kansas State University. After over a decade in the graphic design industry, Deanna discovered jewelry design and quickly fell in love with resin as a medium. Utilizing color, shape and form, Deanna creates wearable graphic design that is forever captured in resin. She currently resides in the Kansas City area.

Pinwheel: round pendant embedded with colored acrylic jewels

70

photograph courtesy of D. Burasco

Gallery
Inspirational Artists

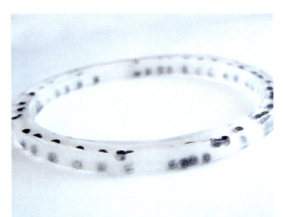

Dotted Black Bangle (cast from hand made mould)

photograph courtesy of D. Burasco

Black Rising: round pendant embedded with black seed beads

photograph courtesy of D. Burasco

Floating Gold Bangle

photograph courtesy of D. Burasco

www.deannaburasco.etsy.com

Gallery
Inspirational Artists

Su Trindle

Long before she started making any, Su was an admirer of contemporary jewellery., haunting galleries and exhibitions wherever she lived from London and Brighton to Sydney and Milan, The mix of precious metals and modern materials expressed in simple, bold sculptural designs fascinated her.

A few years ago she started studying silver jewellery making, in Bath, and set up her business, Quercus Silver. A chance introduction to resin opened new possibilities of color and form, adding a new dimension to her work.

Energy Cufflinks

photograph courtesy of S. Trindle

Gallery
Inspirational Artists

Egg Ring

photograph courtesy of S. Trindle

Spiral Cufflinks

photograph courtesy of S. Trindle

Block Ring

photograph courtesy of S. Trindle

Gallery
Inspirational Artists

Serena Kuhl

Serena studied sculpture for four years at art school, giving her a good grounding in casting and making forms. She spends most of her time as a senior school art teacher, but focuses as much of her time as possible outside the classroom practicing her own art, of which jewellery making is a recent development.

Zen Pebble Garden Bangle

photograph courtesy of S. Kuhl

Sea Anemone rings

photograph courtesy of S. Kuhl

Sea Urchin Stainless Steel ring

photograph courtesy of S. Kuhl

Lime Green Cell bangle

photograph courtesy of S. Kuhl

Where to buy?

Water clear casting resin

CFS Fibreglass Supplies - www.cfsnet.co.uk
01209 821028
United Downs Industrial Park
Redruth
Cornwall
TR16 5HY

East Coast Fibreglass Supplies - www.ecfibreglasssupplies.co.uk
0191 4975134
Rekendyke Industrial Estate,
South Shields,
Tyne and Wear
NE33 5BZ

Moulding materials, premade moulds and pigments

Alec Tiranti - www.tiranti.co.uk
0845 1232100
3 Pipers Court, Berkshire Drive,
Thatcham
Berkshire,
RG19 4ER

Fred Aldous - www.fredaldous.co.uk
0161 2364224
37 Lever Street,
Manchester
M1 1LW

EMA Model Supplies - www.ema-models.co.uk
01932 228228
Unit 2, Shepperton Business Park
Govett Avenue
Shepperton
TW17 8BA

Resin Obsession - www.resinobsession.com
713-598-0330
17115 Mountain Crest Drive,
Spring,
TX 77379
USA

TOMPS - www.tomps.com
0845 658 6677
220 New Road,
Sutton Bridge,
PE12 9QE

Jewellery findings and components

PJ Beads - www.beads.co.uk
01704 575461
583C Liverpool Road,
Ainsdale,
Southport,
PR8 3LU

Gilcos Beads Direct - beadinguk.com/catalog
029 20216353
19 Firs Avenue
Fairwater
Cardiff
CF5 3TF

Index

A

abrasives   13
acetate   40-41
acrylic   63-65
air   17, 66
air circulation   15
airing cupboard   40, 66
apron   16

B

bangle   37-38
beads   45, 53
bottlecaps   26-27
bubbles   29, 41, 50, 66-67
buffing wheel   20
Burasco, Deanna   70-71

C

cabochons   52
car lacquer spray   14, 27, 30, 34, 38,
    42, 46, 53, 60, 67
catalyst   8-9, 18, 23, 27, 29, 33, 37,
    40, 44, 48, 50, 53, 55-56, 59-
    60, 64, 66
chain   24, 35, 42, 46, 57, 61, 65
chaton   61-62
clamp   24, 27
clingfilm   16
cocktail stick   66
colour   12, 37-38, 59, 64
colourant   12
copper leaf   33
cotton   19-20
craft shop   10
cutter bit   60

D

decal   40
Diamond Coolant   20
disposable cup   10, 16, 17-18, 23, 33,
    37, 44, 49, 55, 59, 64

disposal   16
drill   14, 20, 27, 30, 35, 42, 46, 56,
    60-61, 64-65
dropper bottle   18
dust particles   19
dye   10, 12-13, 37, 64
    liquid   12
    opaque   12-13
    paste   12-13
    pearlescent   12, 59
    transparent   12-13

E

earrings   33, 35
Easy Cast   8
eBay   10
embossing powder   13
Envirotex Lite   8

F

fabric   29
face mask   9, 15
    dust mask   15, 19
    ventilator   15
file   13, 19, 34, 53, 64-65
flat lap grinder   19
fibreglassing   9, 13
freezer   66
fumes   15, 48

G

gelcoat   9, 52-53, 56, 60-61, 67
glitter   13, 45
glue   26
gold leaf   33

H

hand cream   19
hardener   8
heat gun   66

I
ice   55
ice cube tray   12, 30, 34

J
jewellers' rouge   65
jump ring   14, 31, 34-35, 42, 46, 57,
          61, 65

K
keyring   26-27
kidney wire   35
kitchen scales   17
Kuhl, Serena   49, 74-75

L
layering   43-44, 67
linseed oil   19
lolly sticks   10, 23, 29, 33, 37, 52, 55-
          56, 59

M
magic tape   63-65
measuring cup   18
microwave   48
mixing   17
Milliput   49
model   49
mould   12, 29-30, 33-34, 37-38, 40-41,
          44-45, 48-50, 52-53, 59-60
      latex   12
      polyethylene   11
      polypropylene   11
      PVC   48
      rigid   11
      silicone   12, 48-50, 67
mould release   12, 67

N
nail varnish remover   16
necklace   31

O
olive oil   24

P
paperweight   67
peg   35, 42, 46, 57, 61, 67
pendant   30, 33, 35, 40
permanent marker pen   1, 49
piercing saw   63
pigment   9, 10, 13
plastercine   49
pliers   14, 24, 27, 31
plique-a-jour   62
polishing   19-20, 67
polishing wheel   20, 65
polymer clay   49, 53
polystyrene   10
polythene sheeting   16
pot life   18
protection   16

R
resin   10, 15-16, 19, 23, 27, 29-30,
          33-34, 37, 40-41, 44-45, 50, 52,
          57, 59, 64-65, 66-67
      bio   67
      doming   8
      epoxy   8-9
      polyester   8-9, 15
ribbon   31
ribbon clamps   31
ring   49-50, 56

S
sanding   19
sandpaper   19, 30, 34, 38, 41, 46, 60
          wet and dry   13, 14, 38,
          65
Scott, Jasmine   68-69
sequins   53
shell   23-24
shrinkage   8
silica gel   67
silver leaf   33
soap   16
sponge   20
starfish   23
steel wool   19

sticker 44
storage 16
sunlight 16
super glue 31, 35, 42, 46, 57, 61
syringe 18

T
tackiness 66
T-Cut 19
Trindle, Su 72-73
tupperware 48
tweezers 61

V
vaseline 67
vice 56, 63
Vinamould 48, 52

W
water 17, 38, 40-41, 46, 49-50, 67
white spirit 67

Z
ziplock bag 66